Watergate

American history, Volume 13

Michael Johnson

Published by Harmony House Publishing, 2024.

While every precaution has been taken in the preparation of this book, the publisher assumes no responsibility for errors or omissions, or for damages resulting from the use of the information contained herein.

WATERGATE

First edition. April 5, 2024.

ISBN: 979-8224506248

Written by Michael Johnson.

Table of Contents

"To those who value transparency, integrity, and the resilience
of democracy,

This book is dedicated to the tireless pursuit of truth and justice, embodied by the journalists, investigators, and individuals who sought to uncover the truth behind the Watergate scandal. To the countless voices who refused to accept corruption and secrecy in government, and who stood up for accountability and the rule of law.

May the lessons of Watergate serve as a reminder of the importance of vigilance and integrity in our democracy, and may we continue to uphold these values in the face of adversity.

With deepest respect and admiration,

Michael Johnson"

Chapter 1: The Break-In

:

The Watergate scandal, perhaps the most infamous political scandal in American history, began with a seemingly ordinary break-in. On June 17, 1972, five men were apprehended by police while attempting to bug the offices of the Democratic National Committee (DNC) at the Watergate complex in Washington, D.C. Little did they know, their actions would set off a chain of events that would shake the foundations of the Nixon administration and redefine the relationship between the government and the press.

Background:

To understand the significance of the Watergate break-in, it's essential to delve into the backgrounds of the individuals involved and their connections to the Nixon administration.

1.1 The Burglars:

The five men arrested at the Watergate complex were: Bernard Barker, Virgilio González, Eugenio Martínez, Frank Sturgis, and James W. McCord Jr. While initially portrayed as bungling burglars, it soon became apparent that they were not acting alone.

Bernard Barker, a Cuban exile, had ties to the Central Intelligence Agency (CIA) and had been involved in previous anti-Castro activities. Virgilio González, another Cuban exile, had worked alongside Barker in anti-Castro efforts. Eugenio Martínez was a former CIA agent who had served in various covert operations. Frank Sturgis, like Barker and González, was a veteran of anti-Castro activities and had connections to the CIA. James W. McCord Jr. was a former CIA officer and security coordinator for the Committee to Re-elect the President (CRP), known colloquially as CREEP.

1.2 The Plumbers:

While the five burglars may have been the ones caught in the act, they were just a small part of a larger operation. Behind the break-in was a secretive group known as the "plumbers," whose primary purpose was to stop leaks of classified information and discredit Nixon's political enemies. Led by E. Howard Hunt and G. Gordon Liddy, both former CIA operatives, the plumbers operated under the direction of John Ehrlichman, one of Nixon's closest advisers.

1.3 The Nixon Administration:

At the center of the Watergate scandal was President Richard Nixon, who had been re-elected in a landslide victory just months before the break-in. Nixon, a shrewd and politically astute leader, had built a reputation as a tough anti-communist during the Cold War. However, beneath his outward image of strength and competence lay a deeply paranoid and insecure man who was willing to go to great lengths to maintain power.

Key Figures in the Nixon Administration:

- Richard Nixon: 37th President of the United States, known for his combative political style and secretive nature.

- John Ehrlichman: Nixon's domestic policy adviser and one of the architects of the Watergate cover-up.

- H.R. Haldeman: Nixon's chief of staff and one of his closest confidants, heavily involved in the Watergate scandal.

- John Dean: White House counsel who would later become a key witness against Nixon, revealing the extent of the cover-up.

The Watergate Break-In:

At 2:30 a.m. on June 17, 1972, security guard Frank Wills noticed tape covering the locks on several doors at the Watergate complex, signaling a potential break-in. Wills contacted the police, who arrived on the scene and apprehended the five burglars inside the DNC headquarters.

The burglars were found in possession of electronic surveillance equipment, cameras, and burglary tools. Initially, the break-in was dismissed as a routine burglary, but as investigators delved deeper, they uncovered evidence linking the burglars to the Nixon administration.

Connections to the Nixon Administration:

While the burglars claimed they were acting alone, it soon became apparent that they had ties to the Nixon administration. Bernard Barker's phone number was found in the address book of E. Howard Hunt, a former CIA operative and White House consultant. Additionally, a check for $25,000 made out to one of the burglars was traced back to the CRP, further implicating the Nixon campaign in the break-in.

The revelation of these connections set off alarm bells in Washington and sparked widespread speculation about the true motives behind the break-in. Was it a botched burglary, or was there something more sinister at play?

Conclusion:

The break-in at the Watergate complex may have seemed like a minor incident at the time, but it would ultimately lead to the downfall of a president. As investigators unraveled the web of lies and deception surrounding the break-in, they uncovered a vast conspiracy orchestrated by the highest levels of the Nixon administration. What began as a simple burglary would soon escalate into a full-blown political scandal that would rock the nation to its core.

Chapter 2: Unraveling the Conspiracy

Investigative journalism has often been hailed as the fourth estate, a crucial check on the powers that be in a democratic society. Nowhere was this more evident than in the Watergate scandal, where the relentless pursuit of the truth by two young reporters at The Washington Post played a pivotal role in exposing the conspiracy that had engulfed the Nixon administration.

2.1 The Rise of Woodward and Bernstein:

Bob Woodward and Carl Bernstein were both relatively inexperienced reporters when they were assigned to cover the Watergate break-in for The Washington Post. Woodward, a former naval officer, had only been at the paper for a year, while Bernstein, a college dropout turned journalist, was known for his tenacity and sharp investigative skills.

Their partnership was an unlikely one - Woodward, the reserved and methodical reporter, complemented Bernstein's brash and confrontational style. Together, they formed a formidable team that would go on to uncover one of the biggest political scandals in American history.

2.2 Following the Money:

From the outset, Woodward and Bernstein were struck by the peculiarities surrounding the Watergate break-in. Why would seasoned political operatives be caught red-handed breaking into the offices of the Democratic National Committee? What were they looking for, and who had sent them?

Their investigation led them down a rabbit hole of secret campaign slush funds, hush money payments, and clandestine meetings in darkened parking garages. At the heart of it all was the Committee to Re-elect the President (CRP), better known as CREEP, and its ties to the White House.

2.3 Deep Throat:

One of the most enduring mysteries of the Watergate scandal was the identity of Woodward and Bernstein's infamous source, known only as Deep Throat. Meeting in the shadowy confines of a parking garage, Deep Throat provided the reporters with invaluable guidance and insider information that would help unravel the conspiracy at the heart of the Nixon administration.

For years, Deep Throat's identity remained a closely guarded secret, fueling speculation and conspiracy theories. It wasn't until 2005, more than 30 years after Watergate, that former FBI Deputy Director Mark Felt revealed himself as the elusive Deep Throat, confirming what many had long suspected.

2.4 Connecting the Dots:

As Woodward and Bernstein continued to dig deeper, they uncovered a web of corruption and deceit that stretched from the White House to the highest levels of the Nixon administration. They traced the flow of illegal campaign funds, exposed the dirty tricks and sabotage tactics employed by Nixon's operatives, and revealed the extent of the cover-up orchestrated by the president himself.

Their reporting sent shockwaves through Washington and captured the imagination of the American public. With each new revelation, the walls of denial erected by the Nixon administration began to crumble, exposing the truth beneath.

2.5 The White House's Response:

As Woodward and Bernstein's reporting gained momentum, the Nixon administration launched a concerted effort to discredit their work and undermine their credibility. Press Secretary Ron Ziegler dismissed their reporting as "a third-rate burglary attempt" and accused the media of engaging in a witch hunt against the president.

Behind the scenes, Nixon's aides waged a covert campaign of intimidation and harassment against the reporters, tapping their phones, spreading false rumors, and even plotting to physically harm them. But

Woodward and Bernstein refused to be intimidated, continuing their investigation with dogged determination and unwavering resolve.

2.6 The Turning Point:

The turning point in Woodward and Bernstein's investigation came with the discovery of the White House tapes - secret recordings made by Nixon of his conversations in the Oval Office. These tapes provided irrefutable evidence of Nixon's involvement in the cover-up and laid bare the extent of his complicity in the Watergate scandal.

Armed with this damning evidence, Woodward and Bernstein published a series of articles that laid out the case against Nixon in stark detail. Their reporting not only forced Nixon to resign in disgrace but also reaffirmed the power of the press to hold those in power accountable for their actions.

Conclusion:

The unraveling of the Watergate conspiracy was a triumph of investigative journalism and a testament to the power of the press to expose corruption and wrongdoing. Through their tireless efforts, Woodward and Bernstein exposed the truth behind the break-in at the Watergate complex and brought down a president in the process. Their reporting remains a shining example of the vital role that a free and independent press plays in a democratic society.

Chapter 3: The Cover-Up Begins

As the investigative efforts of journalists like Bob Woodward and Carl Bernstein began to close in on the truth behind the Watergate break-in, the Nixon administration found itself facing a dilemma. How could they conceal their involvement in the burgeoning scandal and protect the president from the growing tide of public outrage? Thus began one of the most audacious cover-ups in American political history.

3.1 Nixon's Paranoia:

From the outset, Richard Nixon was consumed by a deep-seated paranoia that his political enemies were out to get him. This paranoia would ultimately drive many of the decisions made by the Nixon administration during the Watergate scandal, leading to a series of ill-fated attempts to cover up their involvement in the break-in.

Nixon's obsession with secrecy and control was legendary. He kept detailed records of his conversations in the Oval Office, recorded on a secret tape-recording system installed in the White House. These tapes would later become a central piece of evidence in the Watergate investigation, providing damning proof of Nixon's complicity in the cover-up.

3.2 The Plumbers:

At the heart of the cover-up effort was a secretive group known as the "plumbers." Formed in response to a series of damaging leaks of classified information to the press, the plumbers were tasked with stopping leaks and silencing Nixon's critics by any means necessary.

Led by former CIA operatives E. Howard Hunt and G. Gordon Liddy, the plumbers operated outside the bounds of normal government oversight, engaging in a wide range of illegal activities, including burglary, wiretapping, and sabotage.

The creation of the plumbers unit marked a turning point in the Watergate scandal, as Nixon and his top advisers sought to contain the damage caused by the break-in and prevent further revelations that could threaten the administration's survival.

3.3 The Hunt for Leakers:

One of the plumbers' first tasks was to identify and neutralize the sources of damaging leaks to the press. Using a combination of surveillance techniques and covert operations, they targeted journalists, government officials, and anyone else suspected of leaking information to the media.

Their efforts were not limited to traditional investigative methods. The plumbers also engaged in more sinister tactics, such as wiretapping, break-ins, and even the planting of false information to discredit Nixon's enemies and sow confusion among his critics.

3.4 The Ellsberg Break-In:

One of the plumbers' most notorious operations was the break-in at the office of Daniel Ellsberg's psychiatrist. Ellsberg, a former military analyst, had leaked the Pentagon Papers, a top-secret study of U.S. involvement in Vietnam, to The New York Times in 1971.

Fearing that Ellsberg possessed further damaging information that could be leaked to the press, the plumbers burglarized the office of Ellsberg's psychiatrist in search of incriminating evidence. The break-in was a brazen violation of Ellsberg's privacy and a clear abuse of government power.

3.5 The Cover-Up Unravels:

Despite their best efforts, the Nixon administration was unable to contain the growing scandal surrounding the Watergate break-in. As Woodward and Bernstein continued to uncover evidence of White House involvement, the pressure on Nixon and his top advisers mounted.

The release of the White House tapes in 1974 provided the smoking gun that prosecutors had been searching for, revealing Nixon's direct involvement in the cover-up and his efforts to obstruct justice. The tapes also exposed the extent of the plumbers' activities and the lengths to which Nixon was willing to go to protect himself from scrutiny.

Conclusion:

The cover-up orchestrated by the Nixon administration was a desperate attempt to conceal the truth and preserve the president's grip on power. But in the end, their efforts only served to deepen the scandal and hasten Nixon's downfall. The plumbers' illegal activities exposed the dark underbelly of Nixon's presidency and shattered the illusion of his invincibility. As the cover-up unraveled, it became clear that no one, not even the president of the United States, was above the law.

Chapter 4: Congressional Investigations Begin

As the Watergate scandal continued to unfold, the American public demanded answers. What had happened at the Watergate complex on that fateful night? Who was responsible? And perhaps most importantly, what did President Nixon know, and when did he know it? To uncover the truth, Congress launched a series of investigations that would ultimately lead to the downfall of a president.

4.1 The Senate Watergate Committee:

In February 1973, the Senate established the Select Committee on Presidential Campaign Activities, better known as the Senate Watergate Committee, to investigate the Watergate break-in and related activities. Chaired by Senator Sam Ervin, a folksy and respected lawmaker from North Carolina, the committee was tasked with conducting a thorough and impartial inquiry into the scandal.

The Senate Watergate Committee quickly became the focal point of the investigation, holding televised hearings that captivated the nation and drew millions of viewers. The hearings provided a forum for key witnesses to testify under oath about their knowledge of the Watergate affair and shed light on the inner workings of the Nixon administration.

4.2 The House Judiciary Committee:

In May 1973, the House of Representatives established the Judiciary Committee to investigate whether there were grounds to impeach President Nixon for his role in the Watergate cover-up. Chaired by Congressman Peter Rodino, a seasoned lawmaker from New Jersey, the Judiciary Committee conducted its investigation behind closed doors, gathering evidence and interviewing witnesses in preparation for impeachment proceedings.

The Judiciary Committee's investigation ran parallel to the Senate Watergate Committee's inquiry, with both committees working independently to uncover the truth about Nixon's involvement in the scandal. While the Senate focused on the broader aspects of the Watergate affair, the House Judiciary Committee focused specifically on Nixon's conduct and whether it warranted impeachment.

4.3 Testimony from Key Witnesses:

One of the most dramatic moments of the Senate Watergate Committee hearings came when John Dean, the White House counsel, took the stand to testify about his knowledge of the cover-up. Dean, who had initially been one of Nixon's staunchest defenders, stunned the nation with his revelations about the extent of the conspiracy and the president's involvement in orchestrating the cover-up.

Dean's testimony implicated several top White House officials, including Chief of Staff H.R. Haldeman and Domestic Affairs Adviser John Ehrlichman, in the cover-up and raised serious questions about Nixon's own role in the scandal. His testimony provided a roadmap for investigators as they continued to unravel the web of deception surrounding Watergate.

Another pivotal moment came when Alexander Butterfield, a former aide to President Nixon, revealed the existence of a secret taping system in the White House during his testimony before the Senate Watergate Committee. Butterfield's revelation sent shockwaves through Washington and provided prosecutors with the evidence they needed to subpoena the tapes and prove Nixon's complicity in the cover-up.

4.4 The Smoking Gun:

In July 1974, the Judiciary Committee voted to approve three articles of impeachment against President Nixon: obstruction of justice, abuse of power, and contempt of Congress. The articles were based on the evidence gathered during the committee's investigation, including testimony from key witnesses and the White House tapes.

The turning point came when the Supreme Court ordered Nixon to release the tapes to special prosecutor Leon Jaworski, who discovered a recording of a conversation in which Nixon discussed using the CIA to obstruct the FBI's investigation into the Watergate break-in. This "smoking gun" evidence proved beyond a doubt that Nixon had been involved in the cover-up from the beginning and ultimately led to his resignation.

Conclusion:

The congressional investigations into the Watergate scandal were a watershed moment in American history, demonstrating the power of Congress to hold the president accountable for his actions. Through their meticulous and exhaustive inquiries, the Senate Watergate Committee and the House Judiciary Committee uncovered the truth about Nixon's involvement in the cover-up and paved the way for his resignation. The hearings were a testament to the principles of transparency and accountability that lie at the heart of American democracy, and they serve as a reminder of the importance of checks and balances in ensuring that no one is above the law.

Chapter 5: The Smoking Gun Tape

The release of the White House tapes containing recordings of President Richard Nixon's conversations in the Oval Office was a pivotal moment in the Watergate scandal. Among these recordings was the infamous "smoking gun" tape, which provided irrefutable evidence of Nixon's involvement in the cover-up of the Watergate break-in. The release of this tape ignited a firestorm of public outrage and demands for Nixon's resignation.

5.1 The White House Tapes:

Beginning in 1971, President Nixon secretly recorded thousands of hours of conversations in the Oval Office, as well as in other rooms of the White House. These recordings were made using a sophisticated tape-recording system installed in the president's offices and were intended to provide Nixon with a comprehensive record of his presidency.

Unbeknownst to Nixon, these tapes would become the focal point of the Watergate investigation and ultimately seal his fate. The tapes captured Nixon and his top advisers discussing everything from foreign policy to political strategy to the Watergate scandal itself. They provided a rare glimpse into the inner workings of the Nixon White House and revealed the president's true thoughts and motivations.

5.2 The Smoking Gun Tape:

The "smoking gun" tape refers to a recording of a conversation between Nixon and his chief of staff, H.R. Haldeman, on June 23, 1972, just six days after the Watergate break-in. In the conversation, Nixon can be heard instructing Haldeman to use the Central Intelligence Agency (CIA) to obstruct the Federal Bureau of Investigation's (FBI) investigation into the break-in.

Nixon: "I want you all to stonewall it, let them plead the Fifth Amendment, cover-up, or anything else if it'll save it – save the plan."

This damning evidence proved beyond a doubt that Nixon was complicit in the cover-up from the very beginning and directly implicated him in the obstruction of justice. The release of the smoking gun tape was a turning point in the Watergate scandal, providing prosecutors with the evidence they needed to hold Nixon accountable for his actions.

5.3 Public Outcry and Demands for Nixon's Resignation:

The release of the smoking gun tape sent shockwaves through Washington and the nation at large. For the first time, the American public heard Nixon's own words implicating him in the cover-up of the Watergate break-in. The revelation of Nixon's direct involvement in the scandal sparked a wave of public outrage and demands for his resignation.

Members of Congress from both parties condemned Nixon's actions and called for him to step down. Republican Senator Barry Goldwater, a staunch Nixon supporter, famously told the president that he no longer had the support of his party and that it was time for him to resign.

The public outcry was deafening, with protests erupting across the country and calls for Nixon's impeachment growing louder by the day. Polls showed that a majority of Americans believed Nixon should be impeached and removed from office, as trust in the president and the government reached an all-time low.

5.4 Nixon's Resignation:

Faced with mounting pressure and the near-certainty of impeachment and removal from office, Nixon announced his resignation in a nationally televised address on August 8, 1974. In his speech, Nixon cited the need to spare the country from further division and turmoil as his reason for stepping down.

Nixon: "I have never been a quitter. To leave office before my term is completed is abhorrent to every instinct in my body. But as President, I must put the interest of America first."

With his resignation, Nixon became the first and only president in American history to step down from office. He was succeeded by Vice President Gerald Ford, who would later pardon Nixon for any crimes he may have committed while in office.

Conclusion:

The release of the smoking gun tape and Nixon's subsequent resignation marked the end of a tumultuous chapter in American history. The Watergate scandal exposed the dark underbelly of Nixon's presidency and shattered the illusion of his invincibility. It was a moment of reckoning for the nation, as Americans grappled with the realization that even the president of the United States was not above the law. The legacy of Watergate continues to reverberate to this day, serving as a reminder of the importance of transparency, accountability, and the rule of law in a democratic society.

Chapter 6: Nixon's Reelection and Second Term

Despite the shadow of the Watergate scandal looming over his administration, Richard Nixon embarked on his reelection campaign in 1972 with confidence and determination. The campaign, characterized by its aggressive tactics and emphasis on law and order, culminated in a landslide victory for Nixon and his running mate, Spiro Agnew. However, beneath the surface of Nixon's triumph lay a web of deceit and corruption that would ultimately lead to his downfall.

6.1 The 1972 Presidential Election:

The 1972 presidential election pitted Nixon, the incumbent Republican president, against George McGovern, the Democratic nominee. Nixon ran on a platform of stability and prosperity, touting his achievements in foreign policy and his efforts to end the Vietnam War. He also capitalized on fears of crime and civil unrest, promising to restore law and order to the nation.

The Watergate scandal, which had broken earlier that year, initially seemed to have little impact on Nixon's reelection prospects. His campaign portrayed the scandal as a minor distraction orchestrated by his political enemies and emphasized his strong leadership and experience in office.

Nixon's opponent, George McGovern, struggled to gain traction with voters, facing criticism for his liberal positions on issues such as the Vietnam War and social welfare. The Nixon campaign painted McGovern as a radical extremist and argued that he posed a threat to the nation's security and prosperity.

On Election Day, Nixon won a resounding victory, capturing over 60% of the popular vote and carrying 49 out of 50 states. His landslide victory seemed to vindicate his leadership and put to rest any doubts about his ability to govern.

6.2 Denial and Deflection:

Despite his overwhelming victory, Nixon's second term would be overshadowed by the growing scandal surrounding Watergate. From the outset, Nixon vehemently denied any involvement in the break-in or subsequent cover-up, dismissing the allegations as politically motivated attacks by his opponents.

Nixon: "I am not a crook."

This famous declaration, made during a press conference in November 1973, captured Nixon's defiant stance in the face of mounting evidence of his complicity in the Watergate affair. Despite mounting pressure from the media and Congress, Nixon refused to admit any wrongdoing and continued to assert his innocence.

Meanwhile, Nixon's aides and advisers worked tirelessly to deflect attention away from the scandal and maintain the illusion of normalcy in the White House. They downplayed the significance of the break-in, dismissed it as a "third-rate burglary," and sought to discredit the journalists and investigators who were probing into the affair.

At the same time, Nixon sought to project an image of strength and stability to the American people, emphasizing his accomplishments in foreign policy and his efforts to address domestic issues such as inflation and unemployment. He portrayed himself as a steady hand at the helm of the ship of state, guiding the nation through turbulent times with resolve and determination.

6.3 The Unraveling:

Despite Nixon's efforts to contain the fallout from Watergate, the scandal continued to escalate, fueled by a steady stream of revelations and disclosures. As the Senate Watergate Committee and the House Judiciary Committee conducted their investigations, evidence of Nixon's involvement in the cover-up began to mount.

Key figures in the Nixon administration, including White House counsel John Dean and former Attorney General John Mitchell, were indicted and convicted for their roles in the scandal. Meanwhile, the media's relentless scrutiny of Nixon's actions and statements exposed the inconsistencies and contradictions in his defense.

The turning point came with the release of the White House tapes, which provided incontrovertible evidence of Nixon's complicity in the cover-up. The smoking gun tape, in particular, revealed Nixon's direct involvement in obstructing the FBI's investigation into the Watergate break-in, leading to widespread condemnation and calls for his resignation.

6.4 Nixon's Legacy:

In August 1974, faced with the near-certainty of impeachment and removal from office, Nixon announced his resignation, becoming the first president in American history to do so. His decision to step down marked the end of a tumultuous chapter in American history and brought to a close one of the most notorious political scandals in the nation's history.

Nixon's presidency is now remembered as a cautionary tale of the dangers of unchecked executive power and the corrosive effects of deception and dishonesty in government. His legacy remains deeply tarnished by the Watergate scandal, which exposed the dark underbelly of his administration and shattered the trust of the American people in their government.

Conclusion:

Nixon's reelection and second term were overshadowed by the unfolding Watergate scandal, which ultimately led to his resignation in disgrace. Despite his landslide victory in 1972, Nixon's presidency would be forever tainted by the revelations of corruption and abuse of power that emerged during the Watergate investigation. His refusal to admit wrongdoing and his attempts to cover up the truth only served to deepen the scandal and hasten his downfall. In the end, Nixon's legacy serves as a stark reminder of the importance of accountability, transparency, and the rule of law in preserving the integrity of American democracy.

Chapter 7: Resignations and Indictments

As the Watergate scandal continued to unravel, the Nixon administration found itself besieged by resignations, indictments, and convictions. Top White House aides, including H.R. Haldeman and John Ehrlichman, were forced to resign in disgrace, while members of the Committee to Re-elect the President (CRP) and Nixon's inner circle faced criminal charges and legal consequences for their roles in the cover-up.

7.1 Resignations of H.R. Haldeman and John Ehrlichman:

H.R. Haldeman and John Ehrlichman, two of Nixon's closest advisers and confidants, played key roles in the Watergate cover-up and were among the first casualties of the scandal. Haldeman, Nixon's chief of staff, and Ehrlichman, his domestic affairs adviser, were instrumental in orchestrating the conspiracy to obstruct justice and silence Nixon's political enemies.

In April 1973, amid mounting pressure from Congress and the media, Haldeman and Ehrlichman tendered their resignations to Nixon, who reluctantly accepted them. Their departure marked a significant blow to Nixon's administration and signaled the beginning of the end for the president's inner circle.

The resignations of Haldeman and Ehrlichman sent shockwaves through Washington and fueled speculation about Nixon's own involvement in the Watergate affair. As two of Nixon's most trusted aides, their departure signaled a loss of confidence in the president and raised questions about his ability to govern effectively in the face of mounting scandal.

7.2 Indictments and Convictions:

As the Watergate investigation expanded, a series of indictments and convictions rocked the Nixon administration, implicating members of the CRP and other key figures in Nixon's inner circle. The indictments and convictions laid bare the extent of the conspiracy and exposed the culture of corruption and criminality that had permeated the highest levels of government.

Among those indicted and convicted were:

- John Mitchell: Nixon's former attorney general and head of the CRP, who was indicted on charges of conspiracy, obstruction of justice, and perjury. Mitchell was ultimately convicted and sentenced to prison, becoming the highest-ranking member of the Nixon administration to be incarcerated.

- Jeb Magruder: Deputy director of the CRP, who pleaded guilty to charges of conspiracy and perjury. Magruder's testimony implicated other members of the CRP and provided prosecutors with valuable evidence in their case against Nixon and his aides.

- Charles Colson: Special counsel to President Nixon, who pleaded guilty to charges of obstruction of justice and served time in prison. Colson's involvement in the Watergate scandal tarnished his reputation and ended his political career.

- John Dean: White House counsel who cooperated with prosecutors and provided testimony that implicated Nixon in the cover-up. Dean's decision to cooperate with authorities was a turning point in the Watergate investigation and helped pave the way for Nixon's resignation.

7.3 Fallout and Fallout:

The resignations and indictments of top White House aides and CRP members sent shockwaves through the Nixon administration and rocked the nation to its core. The revelations of corruption and criminality at the highest levels of government shattered the public's trust in the presidency and eroded confidence in the institutions of democracy.

As the Watergate scandal continued to unfold, Nixon's grip on power grew increasingly tenuous, and calls for his resignation grew louder. Members of Congress from both parties called for Nixon to step down, arguing that he had lost the moral authority to govern and that his continued presence in office was a threat to the stability of the nation.

Ultimately, Nixon's resignation in August 1974 marked the culmination of the Watergate scandal and brought an end to one of the darkest chapters in American history. The resignations and indictments of top White House aides and CRP members served as a stark reminder of the importance of accountability and the rule of law in preserving the integrity of American democracy.

Conclusion:

The resignations and indictments of top White House aides and CRP members were a defining moment in the Watergate scandal, signaling the beginning of the end for the Nixon administration. As key figures in Nixon's inner circle fell one by one, the walls of denial and deceit that had shielded the president from accountability began to crumble, exposing the truth beneath. The fallout from the resignations and indictments reverberated throughout the nation, shaking the foundations of government and reaffirming the principles of transparency, accountability, and the rule of law in a democratic society.

Chapter 8: The Saturday Night Massacre

The Saturday Night Massacre stands as one of the most dramatic and controversial moments in American political history. It was a pivotal event in the Watergate scandal that shook the foundations of the Nixon administration and sent shockwaves through the nation. At the center of the controversy was President Richard Nixon's decision to fire Special Prosecutor Archibald Cox and the subsequent resignations of Attorney General Elliot Richardson and Deputy Attorney General William Ruckelshaus. This chapter delves into the events leading up to the Saturday Night Massacre, its immediate aftermath, and its long-lasting impact on American politics.

8.1 The Appointment of Archibald Cox:

In May 1973, amid mounting pressure from Congress and the public, the Nixon administration reluctantly appointed Archibald Cox as special prosecutor to investigate the Watergate scandal. Cox, a respected Harvard law professor and former solicitor general under President John F. Kennedy, was tasked with conducting an independent inquiry into the break-in at the Democratic National Committee headquarters and related matters.

Cox's appointment was seen as a victory for those calling for a thorough and impartial investigation into the Watergate affair. His reputation for integrity and impartiality gave hope to many that the truth would finally be revealed and those responsible for the scandal would be held accountable.

8.2 The Demand for the Tapes:

As Cox's investigation progressed, he quickly honed in on the White House tapes, which he believed held crucial evidence of Nixon's involvement in the cover-up. Cox subpoenaed the tapes, demanding that Nixon turn them over to the special prosecutor's office for review.

Nixon, however, was unwilling to comply with Cox's demands, citing executive privilege and national security concerns. He argued that the tapes were protected by presidential privilege and that he was under no obligation to release them to the special prosecutor.

Cox refused to back down, insisting that the tapes were essential to his investigation and that Nixon had a legal and moral obligation to turn them over. The stage was set for a showdown between the president and the special prosecutor, with the fate of the Watergate investigation hanging in the balance.

8.3 The Saturday Night Massacre:

On the evening of October 20, 1973, Nixon made a fateful decision that would change the course of history. In a move that stunned the nation, he ordered Attorney General Elliot Richardson to fire Cox and abolish the special prosecutor's office.

Richardson, faced with an impossible choice between carrying out Nixon's orders and upholding the rule of law, chose to resign rather than comply with the president's directive. His resignation sent shockwaves through Washington and set off a chain of events that would come to be known as the Saturday Night Massacre.

In a stunning display of principle and integrity, Deputy Attorney General William Ruckelshaus also chose to resign rather than carry out Nixon's orders. With both Richardson and Ruckelshaus out of the picture, Nixon turned to Solicitor General Robert Bork, who reluctantly agreed to carry out the president's wishes and fire Cox.

The firing of Cox and the resignations of Richardson and Ruckelshaus sent shockwaves through Washington and sparked outrage across the country. The events of that fateful night marked a blatant abuse of power by the president and raised serious questions about the integrity of the American justice system.

8.4 The Immediate Aftermath:

The Saturday Night Massacre plunged the Nixon administration into chaos and triggered a constitutional crisis of unprecedented proportions. The firing of Cox and the resignations of Richardson and Ruckelshaus sparked widespread condemnation from members of

Congress, the media, and the public, who saw Nixon's actions as an attack on the rule of law and a blatant attempt to obstruct justice.

In the wake of the massacre, calls for Nixon's impeachment grew louder, with members of Congress from both parties denouncing the president's actions and demanding accountability. The House Judiciary Committee launched an investigation into the events of that night, seeking to uncover the truth behind Nixon's decision to fire Cox and the subsequent resignations of Richardson and Ruckelshaus.

Meanwhile, public support for Nixon continued to erode, as the American people recoiled in horror at the president's flagrant disregard for the principles of democracy and the rule of law. Nixon's approval ratings plummeted, and his credibility was irreparably damaged as the full extent of his involvement in the Watergate scandal came to light.

8.5 The Long-Term Impact:

The Saturday Night Massacre had far-reaching consequences that reverberated throughout American politics for years to come. It exposed the fragility of the American justice system and the dangers of unchecked executive power, highlighting the need for robust checks and balances to prevent abuses of power by the president.

The massacre also galvanized public opposition to Nixon and his administration, paving the way for his eventual resignation less than a year later. It served as a wake-up call to the American people, reminding them of the importance of vigilance and civic engagement in preserving the integrity of their democracy.

In the end, the Saturday Night Massacre marked a dark chapter in American history, but it also served as a testament to the resilience of the American people and their commitment to the principles of justice, accountability, and the rule of law. It remains a cautionary tale of the dangers of authoritarianism and the need to remain ever vigilant in the defense of democracy.

Chapter 9: The Impeachment Proceedings

The impeachment proceedings against President Richard Nixon marked a historic moment in American politics, as Congress grappled with the question of whether to remove a sitting president from office for the first time in the nation's history. The House Judiciary Committee's impeachment inquiry delved into Nixon's conduct during the Watergate scandal, ultimately leading to the adoption of articles of impeachment for obstruction of justice, abuse of power, and contempt of Congress. This chapter explores the events leading up to the impeachment proceedings, the committee's investigation, and the ramifications of its findings.

9.1 Prelude to Impeachment:

In the aftermath of the Saturday Night Massacre, the House Judiciary Committee launched an impeachment inquiry into President Nixon's conduct. The committee, chaired by Congressman Peter Rodino, was tasked with investigating whether there were grounds to impeach Nixon for his role in the Watergate cover-up and related matters.

The impeachment inquiry was a watershed moment in American history, as Congress exercised its constitutional authority to hold the president accountable for his actions. The committee's investigation would ultimately determine whether Nixon had committed high crimes and misdemeanors that warranted removal from office.

9.2 The House Judiciary Committee's Investigation:

The House Judiciary Committee's impeachment inquiry was a lengthy and exhaustive process, spanning months of hearings, testimony, and deliberation. The committee heard from a wide range of witnesses, including former White House aides, journalists, and legal experts, who provided crucial evidence and insight into Nixon's conduct during the Watergate scandal.

Key figures in the Watergate affair, such as John Dean, Alexander Butterfield, and Jeb Magruder, testified before the committee, providing damning evidence of Nixon's involvement in the cover-up and obstruction of justice. Their testimony, coupled with the release of the White House tapes, provided a compelling case for impeachment.

The committee's investigation focused on three main areas of concern: obstruction of justice, abuse of power, and contempt of Congress. These charges stemmed from Nixon's efforts to impede the Watergate investigation, misuse his presidential authority for personal and political gain, and defy congressional oversight of his administration.

9.3 Adoption of Articles of Impeachment:

In July 1974, after months of hearings and deliberation, the House Judiciary Committee voted to approve three articles of impeachment against President Nixon: obstruction of justice, abuse of power, and contempt of Congress. The articles were based on the evidence gathered during the committee's investigation and the findings of its legal staff.

The first article of impeachment charged Nixon with obstruction of justice, alleging that he had engaged in a concerted effort to obstruct the FBI's investigation into the Watergate break-in and cover-up. The second article accused Nixon of abuse of power, alleging that he had misused his presidential authority to intimidate and harass his political opponents. The third article charged Nixon with contempt of Congress, alleging that he had defied congressional subpoenas and obstructed the committee's investigation.

The adoption of articles of impeachment by the House Judiciary Committee marked a significant milestone in the Watergate scandal, as Congress moved one step closer to holding the president accountable for his actions. The committee's decision to impeach Nixon sent shockwaves through Washington and set the stage for a historic showdown in the House of Representatives.

9.4 The Ramifications:

The adoption of articles of impeachment by the House Judiciary Committee set off a political firestorm in Washington and across the country. Calls for Nixon's resignation grew louder, as members of Congress and the public demanded accountability for his actions. The prospect of Nixon becoming the first president in American history to be impeached and removed from office sent shockwaves through the nation and raised serious questions about the stability of the government.

The impeachment proceedings also had profound implications for the presidency and the balance of power between the executive and legislative branches of government. The spectacle of a sitting president facing impeachment for high crimes and misdemeanors tested the resilience of American democracy and raised fundamental questions about the limits of presidential power.

In the end, the House Judiciary Committee's impeachment inquiry laid bare the extent of Nixon's involvement in the Watergate scandal and underscored the importance of accountability and the rule of law in preserving the integrity of American democracy. The committee's findings would set the stage for the next chapter in the Watergate saga: Nixon's resignation and the end of an era in American politics.

Chapter 10: Nixon's Resignation

Richard Nixon's resignation from the presidency on August 8, 1974, marked the culmination of the Watergate scandal and the end of an era in American politics. Nixon's televised resignation speech, delivered from the Oval Office, shocked the nation and brought to a close one of the most tumultuous chapters in American history. Vice President Gerald Ford's ascension to the presidency heralded a new era of leadership, as he sought to heal the wounds of Watergate and restore public trust in the government. This chapter explores the events leading up to Nixon's resignation, the aftermath of his departure, and the challenges facing President Ford as he assumed office in the midst of a national crisis.

10.1 Nixon's Resignation Speech:

On the evening of August 8, 1974, President Richard Nixon addressed the nation in a televised speech from the Oval Office. The speech, delivered with a solemn and somber tone, marked the end of Nixon's presidency and the beginning of a new chapter in American history.

Nixon began his speech by acknowledging the gravity of the moment and the turmoil that had engulfed his administration in the wake of the Watergate scandal. He spoke of the need to put the interests of the nation above his own personal ambitions and to spare the country from further division and turmoil.

Nixon: "I have never been a quitter. To leave office before my term is completed is abhorrent to every instinct in my body. But as President, I must put the interest of America first."

Nixon went on to announce that he would resign from office, effective at noon the following day. He expressed gratitude to the American people for the privilege of serving as their president and asked for their understanding and support during this difficult time.

Nixon: "I would have preferred to carry through to the finish whatever the personal agony it would have involved, and my family unanimously urged me to do so. But the interests of the nation must always come before any personal considerations."

The speech marked the end of Nixon's tumultuous presidency and set the stage for Vice President Gerald Ford's ascension to the presidency.

10.2 Vice President Gerald Ford's Ascension:

With Nixon's resignation, Vice President Gerald Ford assumed the presidency, becoming the 38th president of the United States. Ford, a former congressman from Michigan, was widely regarded as a steady and principled leader with a reputation for integrity and honesty.

Ford's ascension to the presidency marked a turning point in American politics, as he sought to heal the wounds of Watergate and restore public trust in the government. His first priority was to reassure the American people that the nation was in capable hands and that the rule of law would prevail.

Ford: "My fellow Americans, our long national nightmare is over. Our Constitution works; our great Republic is a government of laws and not of men."

Ford wasted no time in taking decisive action to restore confidence in the presidency and rebuild the credibility of the government. He appointed a new attorney general and FBI director to oversee the ongoing investigation into Watergate and vowed to cooperate fully with Congress and the special prosecutor's office.

Ford also took steps to address the economic challenges facing the nation, including inflation and unemployment, and to restore America's standing on the world stage. He traveled abroad to meet with foreign leaders and reassure allies of America's commitment to peace and stability.

10.3 The Fallout from Watergate:

In the aftermath of Nixon's resignation, the nation grappled with the fallout from Watergate and the implications for the future of American democracy. The scandal had exposed deep divisions within the government and eroded public trust in the presidency and the institutions of government.

Congressional investigations into Watergate continued, as lawmakers sought to uncover the full extent of Nixon's involvement in the cover-up and hold accountable those responsible for the abuses of power that had occurred. The release of the White House tapes provided damning evidence of Nixon's complicity in the scandal and fueled calls for further investigation and prosecution.

Meanwhile, the American people struggled to come to terms with the revelations of corruption and criminality that had emerged during the Watergate affair. The scandal had shaken the foundations of American democracy and raised fundamental questions about the integrity of the government and the rule of law.

10.4 Ford's Presidency:

As President Ford settled into office, he faced a daunting set of challenges, both at home and abroad. His administration was tasked with rebuilding public trust in the government, restoring confidence in the presidency, and addressing the pressing issues facing the nation.

Ford's leadership style was characterized by pragmatism and bipartisanship, as he sought to bridge the divide between Democrats and Republicans and unite the country behind a common vision for the future. He worked closely with Congress to enact legislation to address the nation's economic woes and promote social justice and equality.

Ford also made efforts to heal the wounds of Watergate by pardoning Nixon for any crimes he may have committed while in office. The pardon was controversial at the time, but Ford defended his decision as a necessary step to move the country forward and put the bitterness of Watergate behind them.

In the end, Ford's presidency was marked by his efforts to restore integrity and honesty to the White House and to uphold the principles of democracy and the rule of law. Despite the challenges he faced, Ford remained steadfast in his commitment to serving the American people and ensuring a brighter future for the nation.

Conclusion:

Nixon's resignation and Ford's ascension to the presidency marked the end of one of the darkest chapters in American history and the beginning of a new era of leadership. The events of August 8, 1974, served as a stark reminder of the fragility of American democracy and the importance of upholding the rule of law. As the nation grappled with the fallout from Watergate, Ford's presidency offered hope for a brighter future and a renewed commitment to the principles of integrity, honesty, and accountability in government.

Chapter 11: Fallout and Pardon

The fallout from Richard Nixon's resignation and Gerald Ford's pardon of him reverberated throughout the nation, shaping public opinion, testing the limits of executive power, and leaving an indelible mark on American politics. This chapter explores the public reaction to Nixon's resignation and Ford's pardon, examines Ford's rationale for pardoning Nixon, and assesses the impact of the pardon on Ford's presidency.

11.1 Public Reaction to Nixon's Resignation:

The public reaction to Richard Nixon's resignation on August 8, 1974, was mixed, reflecting the deep divisions within the nation over the Watergate scandal and its implications for the presidency. While many Americans welcomed Nixon's departure as a necessary step to restore integrity to the White House and rebuild public trust in the government, others saw it as a tragic end to a presidency marred by scandal and corruption.

In the immediate aftermath of Nixon's resignation, there was a sense of relief and catharsis among the American people, as the nation began to turn the page on one of the darkest chapters in its history. But there was also a sense of disillusionment and betrayal, as the full extent of Nixon's involvement in the Watergate cover-up became clear.

For some, Nixon's resignation represented a triumph of justice and the rule of law, a testament to the resilience of American democracy in the face of corruption and abuse of power. For others, it was a sobering reminder of the fragility of democracy and the dangers of unchecked executive power.

11.2 Ford's Pardon of Nixon:

Just one month after assuming the presidency, Gerald Ford stunned the nation by granting a full and unconditional pardon to Richard Nixon for any crimes he may have committed while in office. Ford's decision to pardon Nixon was met with outrage and controversy, as many Americans questioned the wisdom and fairness of absolving the disgraced former president of his wrongdoing.

Ford's rationale for pardoning Nixon was twofold. First, he believed that a prolonged legal battle over Nixon's involvement in Watergate would further divide the nation and distract from the pressing issues facing the country. He feared that a protracted investigation and trial would paralyze the government and undermine public confidence in the presidency and the institutions of government.

Second, Ford argued that a pardon was necessary to bring closure to the Watergate scandal and allow the nation to move forward. He believed that Nixon had suffered enough and that it was time to put the bitterness of Watergate behind them and focus on the challenges ahead.

Ford: "My conscience tells me clearly and certainly that I cannot prolong the bad dreams that continue to reopen a chapter that is closed."

Ford's decision to pardon Nixon was met with a firestorm of criticism from both Democrats and Republicans, who accused him of betraying the principles of justice and accountability. Many Americans saw the pardon as a politically motivated act of self-preservation, designed to protect Ford and the Republican Party from the fallout of Watergate.

11.3 Fallout from the Pardon:

The pardon of Richard Nixon had far-reaching consequences that reverberated throughout American politics for years to come. The decision sparked outrage among many Americans, who saw it as a miscarriage of justice and a betrayal of the principles of democracy and the rule of law.

Critics argued that the pardon sent a dangerous message that those in positions of power were above the law and immune from accountability for their actions. They accused Ford of putting the interests of the political elite ahead of the interests of the American people and undermining the credibility of the presidency.

The fallout from the pardon tarnished Ford's reputation and damaged his standing with the American people. His approval ratings plummeted, and he faced widespread criticism from both Democrats and Republicans for his decision to pardon Nixon.

In the years that followed, Ford struggled to overcome the stigma of the pardon and regain the trust of the American people. Despite his efforts to address the pressing issues facing the nation, including inflation, unemployment, and foreign policy challenges, his presidency was overshadowed by the specter of Watergate and the controversy surrounding the pardon.

11.4 Legacy of the Pardon:

The pardon of Richard Nixon remains one of the most controversial and divisive acts in American political history. It sparked a national debate over the limits of executive power, the importance of accountability in government, and the role of forgiveness in the pursuit of justice.

For some, the pardon was a necessary and pragmatic decision to heal the wounds of Watergate and allow the nation to move forward. They argued that Ford's actions helped to restore stability and confidence in the presidency and prevented further division and turmoil.

For others, however, the pardon was a stain on the integrity of the presidency and a betrayal of the principles of justice and accountability. They saw it as a blatant abuse of power and a failure of leadership, which undermined the credibility of the government and eroded public trust in the institutions of democracy.

In the end, the pardon of Richard Nixon remains a controversial and polarizing chapter in American history, a reminder of the complexities and challenges of governance in a democracy. It serves as a cautionary tale of the dangers of unchecked executive power and the importance of upholding the rule of law, even in the face of political pressure and public opinion.

Chapter 12: Legacy of Watergate

The Watergate scandal left an indelible mark on American politics and society, reshaping the landscape of governance, media, and public trust in profound and lasting ways. In the aftermath of the scandal, a series of reforms were enacted to address the systemic issues exposed by Watergate, including campaign finance regulations and government transparency laws. Additionally, Watergate had a profound impact on public trust in government and the media, eroding confidence in the institutions of democracy and fostering a culture of skepticism and cynicism. This chapter explores the legacy of Watergate, examining the reforms enacted in its aftermath and assessing its impact on public perception of government and the media.

12.1 Reforms Enacted After Watergate:

In the wake of the Watergate scandal, Congress moved swiftly to enact a series of reforms aimed at restoring integrity and transparency to the political process and preventing similar abuses of power in the future. These reforms addressed a wide range of issues, including campaign finance, government ethics, and oversight of the executive branch.

One of the most significant reforms enacted in the aftermath of Watergate was the Federal Election Campaign Act (FECA) of 1974. FECA imposed strict regulations on campaign contributions and expenditures, requiring candidates and political parties to disclose their fundraising activities and adhere to spending limits. The law also established the Federal Election Commission (FEC) to enforce campaign finance laws and oversee elections.

Another key reform was the Ethics in Government Act of 1978, which established the Office of Government Ethics (OGE) and required government officials to disclose their financial holdings and potential conflicts of interest. The law also created a system of independent counsels to investigate allegations of wrongdoing by high-ranking officials in the executive branch.

Additionally, Watergate spurred efforts to increase transparency and accountability in government, leading to the passage of the Freedom of Information Act (FOIA) in 1974. FOIA gave the public the right to access government records and documents, promoting openness and accountability in government operations.

12.2 Impact on Public Trust in Government:

One of the most enduring legacies of Watergate was its impact on public trust in government. The scandal shattered the illusion of presidential invincibility and exposed the dark underbelly of executive power, eroding confidence in the integrity and honesty of elected officials.

In the years following Watergate, public trust in government plummeted to historic lows, as Americans grappled with the realization that their leaders were capable of deceit and corruption. Surveys conducted during this period showed a dramatic decline in public confidence in the presidency, Congress, and other branches of government.

The legacy of Watergate also had a profound impact on American politics, giving rise to a culture of skepticism and cynicism that persists to this day. Many Americans came to view politicians with suspicion and mistrust, believing that they were more interested in serving their own interests than the public good.

12.3 Impact on Public Trust in the Media:

Watergate also had a profound impact on public trust in the media, as journalists played a central role in uncovering the truth behind the scandal and holding those responsible to account. The investigative reporting of journalists such as Bob Woodward and Carl Bernstein of The Washington Post helped to expose the corruption and criminality at the heart of the Nixon administration, earning them the Pulitzer Prize and cementing their place in history.

However, the media's role in the Watergate scandal also sparked controversy and debate, as critics accused journalists of bias and sensationalism in their coverage of the affair. Some Americans questioned the motives of the media and the integrity of their reporting, leading to a decline in public trust in the press.

Despite these criticisms, Watergate served as a watershed moment for American journalism, reaffirming the importance of a free and independent press in holding those in power accountable and exposing wrongdoing. The legacy of Watergate continues to shape the relationship between the media and the government, reminding us of the vital role that journalists play in preserving the integrity of American democracy.

12.4 Continuing Relevance of Watergate:

Nearly five decades after the Watergate scandal, its legacy remains as relevant as ever, serving as a cautionary tale of the dangers of unchecked executive power and the importance of transparency and accountability in government. The reforms enacted in the aftermath of Watergate have helped to strengthen the democratic process and prevent similar abuses of power in the future.

However, the lessons of Watergate are not confined to the past; they continue to resonate in the present, as the nation grapples with new challenges to its democratic institutions and norms. The erosion of public trust in government and the media, the rise of political polarization, and the proliferation of disinformation and conspiracy theories all serve as reminders of the fragility of American democracy and the need to remain vigilant in its defense.

In the end, the legacy of Watergate serves as a reminder of the enduring values and principles that underpin American democracy: accountability, transparency, and the rule of law. As we confront the challenges of the 21st century, we would do well to heed the lessons of Watergate and reaffirm our commitment to these fundamental ideals, ensuring that the mistakes of the past are not repeated in the future.

Chapter 13: Nixon's Later Years

Following his resignation from the presidency in the wake of the Watergate scandal, Richard Nixon embarked on a journey of personal and professional redemption, seeking to rehabilitate his tarnished image and secure his place in history. Despite the stain of Watergate, Nixon remained a complex and enigmatic figure, whose later years were marked by a mixture of triumphs and setbacks, as he grappled with his legacy and sought to rebuild his reputation. This chapter explores Nixon's attempts at rehabilitation, including his efforts to write his memoirs, and examines the legacy and public perception of Nixon in the years following Watergate.

13.1 Nixon's Attempts at Rehabilitation:

In the aftermath of Watergate, Richard Nixon faced the daunting task of rebuilding his reputation and restoring his place in American society. Determined to reclaim his legacy, Nixon embarked on a series of initiatives aimed at rehabilitating his image and securing his place in history.

One of Nixon's most ambitious projects was the writing of his memoirs, a comprehensive account of his life and political career. Titled "RN: The Memoirs of Richard Nixon," the book was published in 1978 and became an instant bestseller, earning praise for its candid and introspective portrayal of Nixon's life and presidency.

In his memoirs, Nixon sought to provide his own version of events surrounding Watergate, offering insights into his motivations and actions during the crisis. While some critics dismissed the book as a self-serving attempt to rewrite history, others praised Nixon for his honesty and candor in addressing the controversies and challenges of his presidency.

In addition to writing his memoirs, Nixon embarked on a series of speaking engagements and public appearances, seeking to engage with the American people and present himself as a statesman and elder statesman. Despite facing criticism and hostility from some quarters, Nixon remained undeterred in his efforts to rehabilitate his image and secure his place in history.

13.2 Legacy and Public Perception of Nixon Post-Watergate:

Despite his efforts at rehabilitation, Richard Nixon's legacy remained deeply controversial and divisive in the years following Watergate. For many Americans, Nixon would always be synonymous with corruption, deceit, and abuse of power, tarnishing his reputation and undermining his accomplishments as president.

However, Nixon's legacy was not without its defenders, who argued that he was unfairly vilified by his critics and that his contributions to American politics and foreign policy deserved recognition. They pointed to Nixon's achievements in opening diplomatic relations with China, negotiating arms control agreements with the Soviet Union, and ending American involvement in the Vietnam War as evidence of his statesmanship and leadership.

In the decades following Watergate, public perception of Nixon remained deeply polarized, reflecting the enduring legacy of the scandal and the complexities of his presidency. While some Americans continued to view Nixon with disdain and distrust, others saw him as a flawed but ultimately tragic figure, whose downfall was the result of hubris and ambition.

Nixon's later years were marked by a mixture of triumphs and setbacks, as he sought to come to terms with his legacy and find redemption in the eyes of history. Despite his efforts, however, Nixon would never fully escape the shadow of Watergate, which loomed large over his later years and cast a long shadow over his legacy.

13.3 Nixon's Death and Legacy:

Richard Nixon passed away on April 22, 1994, at the age of 81, following a stroke. His death marked the end of an era in American politics and brought to a close one of the most tumultuous chapters in the nation's history.

In the years since his death, Nixon's legacy has undergone a process of reassessment and reevaluation, as historians and scholars have sought to make sense of his complicated and contradictory legacy. While Nixon's achievements in foreign policy and domestic affairs have earned him grudging respect from some quarters, his role in the Watergate scandal continues to overshadow his accomplishments and define his presidency.

Despite his flaws and shortcomings, Richard Nixon remains a towering figure in American politics, whose impact on the nation continues to be felt to this day. His legacy serves as a cautionary tale of the dangers of unchecked executive power and the importance of accountability and transparency in government.

In the end, Nixon's later years were marked by a mixture of triumphs and setbacks, as he sought to come to terms with his legacy and secure his place in history. While his efforts at rehabilitation were met with mixed success, Nixon's legacy remains a subject of debate and controversy, reflecting the complexities and contradictions of his presidency and the enduring legacy of Watergate.

Chapter 14: Lessons Learned

The Watergate scandal stands as a cautionary tale in American history, serving as a stark reminder of the dangers of unchecked power, the erosion of democratic norms, and the importance of accountability and the rule of law in safeguarding the integrity of democratic institutions. As the nation grappled with the fallout from Watergate, it was forced to confront a series of systemic issues that had contributed to the crisis, and to reflect on the lessons learned from this dark chapter in American politics. This chapter analyzes the systemic issues that led to the Watergate scandal and reflects on the importance of accountability and the rule of law in a democracy.

14.1 Analysis of Systemic Issues:

The Watergate scandal was not merely the result of a few bad actors engaging in criminal behavior; rather, it was symptomatic of a broader set of systemic issues that had plagued American politics for decades. At its core, Watergate exposed the corrosive influence of power and the lengths to which politicians would go to protect their interests and maintain their grip on power.

One of the key systemic issues that led to Watergate was the culture of secrecy and impunity that pervaded the Nixon administration. From the outset, Nixon and his closest advisors operated with a sense of entitlement and a belief that they were above the law. This culture of secrecy created a climate of fear and intimidation, where dissent was suppressed and critics were targeted for retribution.

Another systemic issue that contributed to Watergate was the erosion of checks and balances within the government. As the executive branch expanded its powers in the post-World War II era, Congress and the courts struggled to assert their authority and hold the president accountable for his actions. This imbalance of power created opportunities for abuse and corruption, as Nixon and his allies exploited weaknesses in the system to advance their own agenda.

Additionally, the Watergate scandal exposed the influence of money in politics and the corrosive effect of special interests on the political process. Nixon's re-election campaign was awash in dirty money, much of it coming from wealthy donors and corporations seeking to influence government policy for their own benefit. This flood of money corrupted the political process and undermined the integrity of elections, creating an environment ripe for abuse and manipulation.

14.2 Reflections on Accountability and the Rule of Law:

At its heart, the Watergate scandal was a failure of accountability and the rule of law, as those in positions of power sought to evade responsibility for their actions and subvert the mechanisms of democratic governance. The lessons of Watergate remind us of the importance of holding elected officials accountable for their actions and upholding the rule of law as a bulwark against tyranny and corruption.

One of the central lessons of Watergate is the importance of transparency and openness in government operations. The Nixon administration's attempts to conceal its involvement in the Watergate break-in and cover-up were ultimately its undoing, as the truth was slowly but inexorably brought to light through the efforts of journalists, investigators, and whistleblowers. The lesson here is clear: in a democracy, the people have a right to know what their government is doing, and transparency is essential to maintaining public trust and confidence in the institutions of government.

Another lesson of Watergate is the importance of holding elected officials accountable for their actions, regardless of their position or party affiliation. The Watergate scandal demonstrated the power of the checks and balances built into the American system of government, as Congress, the courts, and the media worked together to uncover the truth and hold Nixon and his associates accountable for their crimes. This commitment to accountability and the rule of law is essential to preserving the integrity of democratic institutions and ensuring that those in power are held to account for their actions.

Finally, the lessons of Watergate remind us of the fragility of democracy and the need for constant vigilance in defending its principles and values. The Watergate scandal was a wake-up call for the nation, a reminder that democracy is not a given, but a fragile and precious gift that must be nurtured and protected. As we reflect on the lessons of Watergate, we must renew our commitment to the ideals of accountability, transparency, and the rule of law, and work together to build a more just and equitable society for future generations.

Chapter 15: Watergate's Enduring Impact

The Watergate scandal remains one of the defining moments in American history, casting a long shadow over the nation's political landscape and leaving a lasting imprint on its institutions, culture, and collective memory. As we reflect on the enduring impact of Watergate, we are reminded of the profound lessons learned from this dark chapter in American politics, and the importance of remaining vigilant in defending the principles of democracy, accountability, and the rule of law. This chapter explores Watergate's place in American history, its lasting repercussions, and offers final reflections on the enduring lessons of the scandal.

15.1 Watergate's Place in American History:

Watergate occupies a unique place in American history, serving as a cautionary tale of the dangers of unchecked power and the importance of upholding the rule of law in a democracy. The scandal shook the foundations of the presidency and tested the resilience of American democracy, as the nation grappled with the revelation of corruption and criminality at the highest levels of government.

Watergate exposed a series of systemic issues that had plagued American politics for decades, including the erosion of democratic norms, the influence of money in politics, and the abuse of executive power. The scandal laid bare the corrosive effects of secrecy, deception, and impunity in government, and served as a wake-up call for the nation to confront the systemic flaws that had allowed such abuses to occur.

At its core, Watergate was a story of hubris, betrayal, and redemption, as the nation confronted the dark underbelly of the presidency and sought to hold those responsible to account for their actions. The scandal led to the resignation of President Richard Nixon, the first and only time in American history that a president has been forced to resign from office, and sent shockwaves through the political establishment.

15.2 Watergate's Lasting Repercussions:

The repercussions of Watergate were far-reaching and enduring, shaping the course of American politics and society for decades to come. The scandal led to a series of reforms aimed at restoring integrity and transparency to the political process, including campaign finance regulations, government ethics laws, and increased oversight of the executive branch.

Watergate also had a profound impact on public trust in government and the media, eroding confidence in the institutions of democracy and fostering a culture of skepticism and cynicism. The scandal shattered the illusion of presidential invincibility and exposed the vulnerabilities of the political system to abuse and corruption.

In the years following Watergate, the nation grappled with the legacy of the scandal, as historians and scholars sought to make sense of its impact on American politics and society. While some saw Watergate as a stain on the presidency and a betrayal of the public trust, others viewed it as a necessary reckoning with the abuses of power that had long plagued American politics.

15.3 Conclusion and Final Reflections:

As we look back on the enduring impact of Watergate, we are reminded of the importance of remaining vigilant in defending the principles of democracy, accountability, and the rule of law. The lessons of Watergate are as relevant today as they were in the 1970s, serving as a reminder of the fragility of democracy and the need for constant vigilance in protecting its principles and values.

The enduring legacy of Watergate is a testament to the resilience of American democracy and the commitment of its citizens to upholding the rule of law. Despite the challenges and setbacks we have faced as a nation, we have emerged stronger and more resilient, reaffirming our commitment to the ideals of justice, equality, and freedom.

As we reflect on the lessons of Watergate, let us renew our commitment to building a more just and equitable society, where the principles of democracy, accountability, and the rule of law are upheld and defended. Let us strive to learn from the mistakes of the past and work together to build a brighter future for ourselves and for generations to come. In the end, the enduring legacy of Watergate is not one of scandal and corruption, but of resilience and renewal, as the nation continues its journey toward a more perfect union.

Don't miss out!

Visit the website below and you can sign up to receive emails whenever Michael Johnson publishes a new book. There's no charge and no obligation.

https://books2read.com/r/B-A-OREFB-JEXAD

BOOKS 2 READ

Connecting independent readers to independent writers.

Did you love *Watergate*? Then you should read *The Moon Landing*[1] by Michael Johnson!

[2]

"Experience the awe-inspiring journey of humanity's greatest achievement in 'The Moon Landing: America's Giant Leap for Mankind.' From the intense space race between superpowers to the historic moment Neil Armstrong set foot on the lunar surface, this book takes you through the gripping tale of determination, innovation, and triumph. Delve into the challenges faced by NASA's Apollo program, the exhilarating moments of the Apollo 11 mission, and the lasting impact of mankind's first steps on the moon. Discover the cultural, scientific, and human significance of this monumental event that continues to inspire generations."

---

1. https://books2read.com/u/4DjOxP

2. https://books2read.com/u/4DjOxP

About the Author

Michael Johnson is a distinguished historian specializing in American history. With a degree in History from Harvard University, Johnson's work delves into pivotal moments, figures, and themes shaping the United States. He has authored numerous acclaimed books, offering insightful perspectives and engaging narratives. Johnson's commitment to meticulous scholarship and compelling storytelling has earned him widespread acclaim in the field. Passionate about sharing his expertise, he frequently engages in lectures and public events to foster a deeper appreciation for America's past.